Contents

Any words appearing in bold, **like this**, are explained
in the Glossary.

The chicken

Chickens are birds. Like all birds, they have beaks, wings and feathers. Chickens come in many different colours, including black, orange, brown, red or white. They usually have some floppy skin around their face. Chickens are farmed all over the world. The females are called **hens**. They lay eggs. The males are called **cocks**, or cockerels. They are kept so that the hens can have baby chicks.

These chickens live on a farm in Suffolk, England.

The Life of a
CHICKEN

Clare Hibbert

www.raintreepublishers.co.uk

Visit our website to find out more information about **Raintree** books.

To order:
☎ Phone 44 (0) 1865 888112
🖹 Send a fax to 44 (0) 1865 314091
💻 Visit the Raintree Bookshop at **www.raintreepublishers.co.uk** to browse our catalogue and order online.

First published in Great Britain by Raintree, Halley Court, Jordan Hill, Oxford OX2 8EJ, part of Harcourt Education.
Raintree is a registered trademark of Harcourt Education Ltd.

Editorial: Nick Hunter and Catherine Clarke
Design: Michelle Lisseter and Tipani Design
   (www.tipani.co.uk)
Illustration: Tony Jones, Art Construction
Picture Research: Maria Joannou and Elaine Willis
Production: Jonathan Smith

Originated by Dot Gradations Ltd
Printed and bound in China by South China Printing Company

ISBN 1 844 43301 3 (Hardback)
08 07 06 05 04
10 9 8 7 6 5 4 3 2 1

ISBN 1 844 43308 0 (Paperback)
09 08 07 06 05
10 9 8 7 6 5 4 3 2 1

British Library Cataloguing in Publication Data
Hibbert, Clare
The Life of a Chicken. – (Life Cycles)
571.8'18625
A full catalogue record for this book is available from the British Library.

Acknowledgements
The publishers would like to thank the following for permission to reproduce photographs:
Ardea (P. Morris) p. **12**; Corbis p. **29**; FLPA pp. **4** (E. & D. Hosking), **5** (B. B. Casals), **9** (J. Zimmermann), **11** (Alwyn Roberts), **14** (Foto Natura Stock), **15** (Foto Natura Stock), **16** (Derek Middleton), **17** (Foto Natura Stock), **18** (John Watkins), **19** (Foto Natura Stock), **20** (B. B. Casals), **21** (J. Vermeer/Foto Natura), **22** (John Watkins), **23** (J. Neukampf/JB/Foto Natura), **24** (Tony Hamblin), **25** (Terry Whittaker), **26** (Gerard Lacz), **28** (R. P. Lawrence); Getty Images (Taxi) p. **8**; NHPA (Ernie Janes) p. **27**; Oxford Scientific Films p. **10**; Science Photo Library (Andrew Syred) p. **13**.

Cover photograph of a chick, reproduced with permission of Ardea.

The publishers would like to thank Janet Stott for her assistance in the preparation of this book.

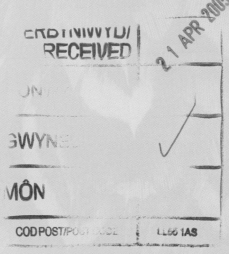

Growing up

Chicks **hatch** out of eggs. Only special eggs hatch into chicks – not the ordinary eggs that you eat. Just as you grow bigger year by year, the chick grows and changes. The different stages of the chicken's life make up its **life cycle**.

Where wild chickens live

Although chickens are farm animals, the first ones were wild. There are still a few wild chickens left. They are called jungle fowl. They live in the jungles of Asia, where they peck the ground for insects, seeds and berries.

These fluffy yellow chicks are less than a week old.

A chicken's life

The **life cycle** of a chicken begins when a **hen mates** with a **cock**. This means that the hen's eggs will be able to **hatch** into chicks. Inside each egg, a baby chick develops.

After the chick hatches, it grows quickly. At first, its feathers are soft and downy, but its stiffer adult feathers start to appear after about a week.

Adult life

The chicken is fully grown at six to eight weeks old. Hens start laying eggs when they are about five or six months old. They are able to mate and produce their own chicks from about eight months old. Hens and cockerels can live for about six years, or even longer.

After they are 22 weeks old, the chickens are adults and can mate.

The **embryo** develops inside the egg for three weeks.

The chick hatches from the egg.

The chick is one week old.

The chicken is five weeks old.

This diagram shows the life cycle of a chicken, from egg to adult.

A place to lay

Hens lay eggs on most days. Usually, hens leave their eggs. They want to peck around with the other hens. Sometimes though, a hen feels **broody**. She wants to sit on her eggs until they **hatch**.

The broody hen collects extra straw to line her nest. Over the next few days, she lays a **clutch** of eggs. She needs to keep the eggs cosy and warm so she sits on them.

This hen is brooding – sitting on her eggs to keep them warm.

Inside story

As long as the hen has **mated** with a **cock**, each egg contains the beginnings of a chick. This is called an **embryo**. There is also egg **yolk**, to feed the growing embryo, and egg white, to provide water and to cushion the embryo inside the shell.

Egg thieves!

Humans are not the only ones that love to eat hen's eggs. So do birds of prey, foxes, raccoons and snakes. They will steal a hen's eggs if they get the chance. Luckily, most hens nest in hen houses. Here, there is a wire fence to keep out foxes and other egg thieves.

This embryo has been growing inside the egg for around two days.

embryo

egg white

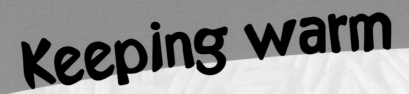

Keeping warm

The **hen** has to keep the eggs warm, otherwise the **embryos** will die. She sits on the eggs almost all day, apart from a short, ten-minute break to eat and drink. Then she returns to the nest.

Sometimes, to make the nest cosier, she plucks out some of her soft chest feathers. She turns her eggs over at least three times a day, so they receive heat all over.

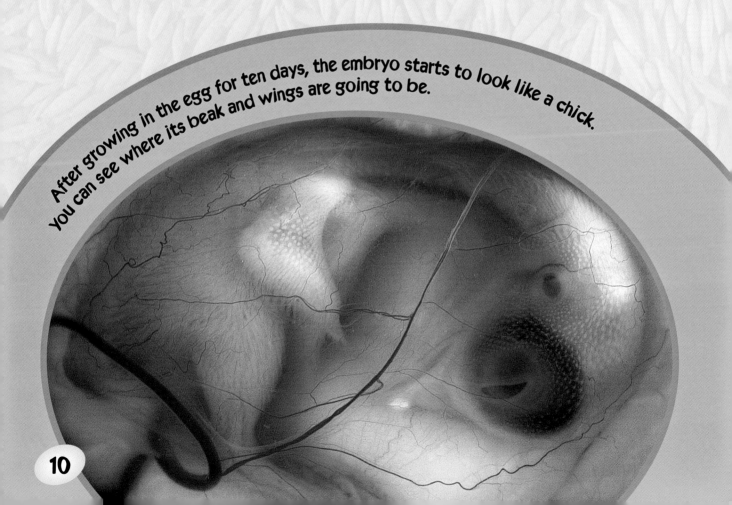

After growing in the egg for ten days, the embryo starts to look like a chick. You can see where its beak and wings are going to be.

Hatchery eggs

On big farms, eggs are taken away from the hens and kept warm in a **hatchery**. This means the mother hen does not have to be busy keeping the eggs warm. Instead, she can keep on laying fresh eggs.

Incubators

The machines that farmers use to hatch eggs are called **incubators**. On big farms, the incubators are enormous. As well as keeping the eggs warm, they also turn the eggs, just as a mother hen would.

Nearly there

For three weeks, the chick **embryo** develops inside the egg. Its eyes start to form at the end of the first day and its heart begins to beat during the second day. The chick's first feathers appear during the second week. At the beginning of the third week, its claws and beak grow hard and firm.

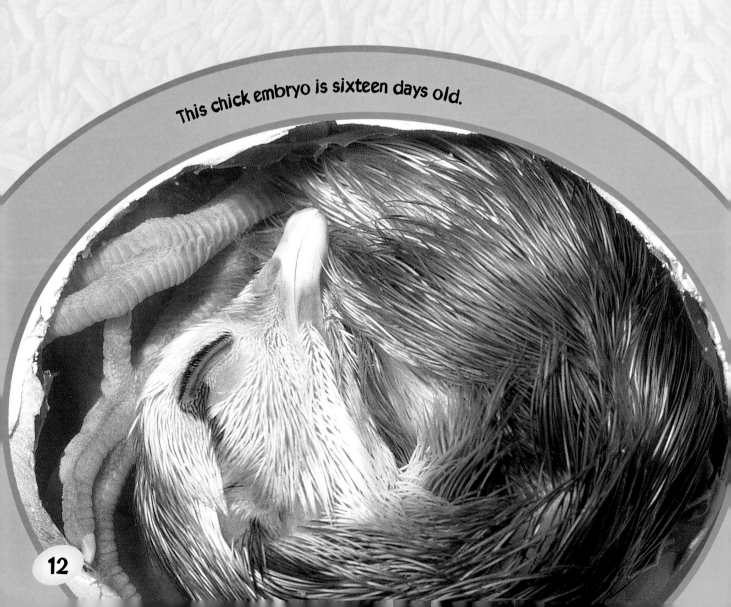

This chick embryo is sixteen days old.

Last days

During the last few days, it is quite a squash for the embryo in the shell. All the remaining egg **yolk** and white is taken into the embryo's body.

Breathing

Like all animals, the developing chick needs air to breathe. The egg has a space at one end, which is filled with air. It also has tiny holes all over its surface that let in fresh air.

This is what a cracked eggshell looks like under a **microscope**. Air passes through the shell, so that the chick inside can breathe.

Hatching Out

Around 20 days after it was laid, a noise comes from the egg. It is the chick cheeping! The next day, it begins to peck at the shell. On top of its beak, the chick has a special **egg tooth** to help it break through the strong shell. Even so, it takes the baby bird almost a whole day to chip its way out.

The hatching chick struggles and pushes to crack the shell.

First appearances

The crumpled chick looks strange when it first comes out of the egg. Its feathers are all wet and its scaly feet look very large for its body.

Shell shield

An eggshell has to bear the weight of a nesting **hen**. It can support up to 4 kilograms before it cracks – that is almost the same weight as about 130 newly hatched chicks! No wonder it takes the chick so long to break out.

Out at last! The newly-hatched chick is tired out.

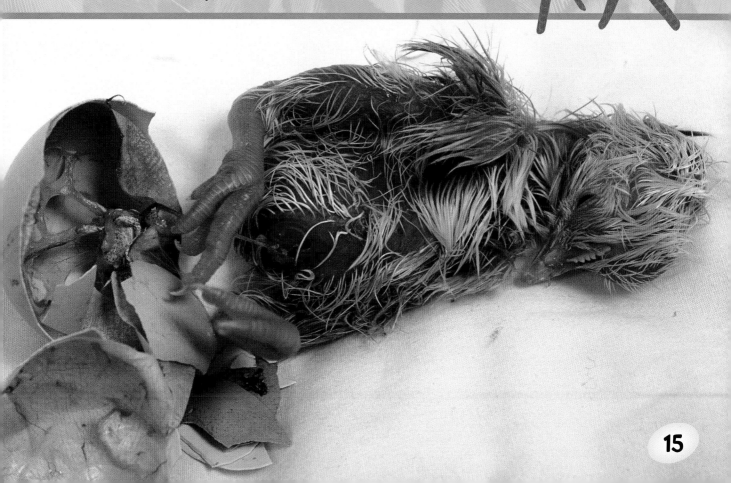

First day

The chick fluffs out its wet feathers and they soon dry out. The feathers are soft and downy, not like an adult chicken's.

The rest of the eggs in the **clutch** have **hatched** at the same time. The chicks stay close to their mother. They are too small to make enough of their own body heat. Without the warmth of the **hen**, they would soon die.

Young chicks stay huddled near to their mother.

Feeling peckish?

The baby chicks do not need to eat or drink anything for the first couple of days. They still have food and water in their tummies, from the egg **yolk** and white.

Cock-a-doodle-doo!

The newly-hatched chicks cheep and chirp so that their mother knows where they are. As adults, the chickens will make a whole range of sounds, including clucks and cackles, crows and whistles, and even cat-like purrs.

The chick opens its tiny beak to chirp for its mother.

First food

After a couple of days, the chicks start eating. They follow their mother and copy what she does, pecking grains or food **pellets** from the ground. In a **hatchery**, they learn to eat special chick food from feeders. Farmers sometimes call this starter food.

Chicks not raised by their mothers still need to be kept warm. Special heat lamps do the job.

Boys and girls

On big farms, the chicks are sorted into males and females. This happens when the birds are about a week old. The females will be raised at the egg farm. When they grow up, they will be kept for laying eggs. Most of the males go to the **broiler** farm, to be fattened for chicken meat.

Grains and grit

Chickens do not have teeth. Along with the **chicken feed**, farmers scatter grit, such as crushed-up oyster shells. The chickens eat the grit along with their food. The grit helps to grind down the food in the gizzard, a part of the chick's stomach.

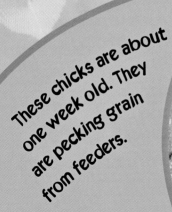

These chicks are about one week old. They are pecking grain from feeders.

First feathers

After a week, the first adult feathers appear on the chick's wings. The bird's body is changing shape, too. It is getting plumper and the neck is getting longer. The feet do not look so enormous.

The first adult feathers appear on the chick's wings when it is one week old.

Looking good

Over the next week, more and more of the chick's body is covered with adult feathers. The chick learns to spend time **preening.** The chick uses its beak to spread oil over its feathers. It collects the oil from a special **oil gland**, at the base of its tail feathers.

Pests

Chickens pick through their feathers to get rid of insect **pests**, such as fleas, mites and lice. Another way is to take a dust bath. The bird gets sand and dirt into its wings, then shakes them out – along with the pests!

When the chicks are around one or two weeks old, they need to preen their feathers to keep them sleek, warm and waterproof.

Free-range chickens

Chicks can start to go outside at about two to three weeks old. Some farmers choose to keep the chicks inside all the time. This is called **battery farming**.

Other farmers prefer to let the chicks outside during the day to roam free. These **free-range** chickens can eat plants and insects as well as **chicken feed**. They also get more exercise than battery chickens so they are healthier and seem happier.

These free-range hens are about six weeks old.

Pecking order

All chickens peck at moving things – which includes other chicks. Sometimes, farmers hang up a cabbage on a string. Hopefully, the chicks will peck at that, instead of each other.

What's a wattle?

Colourful flaps of skin, called the comb and wattles, appear when the chicks are a month old. The wattles are around the beak and the comb is on top of the head. In adult birds, they help to attract a **mate**.

As well as food, growing chicks need water. This chick is standing next to its water feeder, taking a drink.

Broiler chickens

Chickens that are going to be used for meat are called **broilers**. They are usually fed special food, which will help them to put on weight quickly. The plumper the birds, the more meat they will give. Maize is a good, fattening food. Broilers are fully grown at six to eight weeks old.

Free-range broilers can peck around outside. The fence keeps the chickens in – and foxes out.

Hungry hunters

Like all chickens, the birds on broiler farms have to be kept safe from predators – animals that hunt other animals for food. Hungry foxes, hawks and owls will sneak in and snatch a bird if they can. The outside spaces where the birds roam free are carefully covered with chicken wire. There are sturdy fences all around, and the birds are always locked in the broiler sheds at night.

The fox is a type of wild dog. It eats just about anything – including farmer's chickens.

Ready to lay

Young **hens** are called pullets. They start laying eggs when they are about 22 weeks old. They lay in nesting boxes. Farmers gather the eggs so they can be sold for people to eat. The pullet does not lay an egg every single day. She normally lays two eggs every three days.

Now this young hen is grown up enough to lay eggs of her own.

The collected eggs are sorted into trays.

Flying away

Although chickens are birds, not all of them can fly.
Some have been specially **bred** not to. The types that
can fly are usually kept in covered pens.

Another way to stop them escaping is to clip the
flight feathers from one wing. This does not hurt
the birds, but it only lasts until their next moult.
Moulting is when the chicken sheds its feathers.
After moulting, all the bird's feathers grow back,
including the flight feathers.

Special eggs

Most **hens** lay eggs that cannot **hatch** into chicks. The eggs – which are the type we eat – contain a **yolk** and a white, but no **embryo**. This is because the hens have not **mated** with a **cock**. Once she has mated, a hen's next eggs will each contain the tiny beginnings of a chick embryo. They are called fertile eggs.

Farmers usually keep one cock for every ten hens. The cock will mate with all of them.

New life

Not all fertile eggs develop into chicks. This can only happen if the hen **broods** them and keeps them warm – or if the farmer puts the eggs into an **incubator**. Then, the embryos inside the eggs will grow. After three weeks, the new chicks will hatch and the **life cycle** will start all over again.

Hens sit on their eggs almost all day, apart from a short break to eat and drink.

Find out for yourself

The best way to find out more about the **life cycle** of a chicken is to watch it happen with your own eyes. Ask your teacher if your class can go on an outing to a farm.

Books to read

Farm Animals: Chickens, Rachael Bell (Heinemann Library, 2001)
How Do They Grow? From Chick To Chicken, Jillian Powell (Hodder Wayland, 2001)

Using the Internet

Explore the Internet to find out more about chickens. Websites can change, but if some of the links below no longer work, don't worry. Use a search engine, such as www.yahooligans.com, and type in keywords such as 'chicken', 'egg' and 'hatch'.

Websites

http://www.uga.edu/~lam/kids/poultry/plifecycle.html
Photos and words tell the story of a broiler's life.
http://www.poultrymad.co.uk/chicken-facts/index.shtml
Find lots of chicken facts, plus links to pages all about different chicken breeds.

Disclaimer
All the Internet addresses (URLs) given in this book were valid at the time of going to press. However, due to the dynamic nature of the Internet, some addresses may have changed, or sites may have ceased to exist since publication. While the author and publishers regret any inconvenience this may cause readers, no responsibility for any such changes can be accepted by either the author or the publishers.

Glossary

battery farming keeping lots of chickens together inside large hen houses. Battery chickens are never allowed to go outside.

bred when animals are raised by humans

broiler chicken that is raised for its meat. Broilers are usually males.

broody hen that wants to keep her eggs warm until they hatch

chicken feed food for chickens, in the form of grain or pellets

clutch group of eggs

cock male chicken

egg tooth hard, pointy bit on a chick's beak that helps it to break out of the egg. It drops off when the chick is about three days old.

embryo baby animal before it has hatched from an egg, or before it has been born

free-range chicken that is allowed outside the hen house during the day

hatch when a young animal comes out of its egg

hatchery large shed where machines called incubators keep eggs warm until they hatch

hen female chicken

incubator machine that produces heat and is used to hatch eggs

life cycle all the different stages in the life of a living thing, such as an animal or plant

mate (noun) animal that comes together with another animal to make eggs or babies

mate (verb) when a male and female come together to make eggs or babies

microscope instrument used for looking at very small things. Microscopes make things look much bigger.

oil gland also called the preen gland. The area at the base of a chicken's tail feathers that produces oil. The chicken spreads this oil over its feathers when preening, to help keep them waterproof.

pellets dried food for chickens that is pressed into small tube shapes

pest animal that causes trouble for other animals. Fleas are pests because they bite, for example.

preening grooming of a bird's feathers, by running them through its beak

yolk yellowish part of an egg that contains food for the growing embryo

Index